BLACK BALLOONS

I've followed Anthony Seidman's

career for years, and *Black Balloons*, as the title suggests, works from the darkest of his palettes. "Blood fleck on napkin. Wasp floating in a goblet of pinot grigio…sniff the gangrenous. The amputated foot." It's not for mere effect. These anti-paeans take one back to Neruda's "Walking Around" and its moist guts of the earth, in a sustained, low-frequency cry for sanity in the face of political putrefaction. The poet hurts, his "scab is a lake where bull shark flits toward chum." In punchy, clipped poetic prose, he parses out our commonweal psychic pain, each poem a blind alley in which he must retrace his steps to get to the next imagistic manifesto. As always, Seidman is a master of lacerating catalogues, each noun the flick-lash of a whip, regicide the endgame. One can only admire this ferocity in its refusal to offer epiphanies. I had long since given up on the prose poem's efficacy or relevance, but this poet has redeemed the form, imbuing each page with singular, polyvalent prose utterly clear in tone and intention. "I hear a geography in my breathing, jungle beneath each fingernail, vacant lot tart with dust and sunlight, reek of ink and syntax, so foundational, like milk or gladioli."

Johnny Payne, author of *Ostraca*

Blurbs don't exist; they're the products of some carbon meat cleaver's imagination. Therefore I can't speak of Anthony Seidman's *Black Balloons*. It's not my place. A league of original jerboas would vanquish any passive attempt at embracing this verbal octagon. But, boy, this art is within me, within my superior moments of mental tendrilousness. These indecent treasures that pursue themselves are called "Olvera Street's lucid vanadium." No. It's like this: I happened to pass the murdered sun within a tornado one day, as lost as a fanatical lottery ticket. The air dreamed of reaching a candelabra of zeroes. Then Seidman dug into the soil from which you were born, and a siren began to imitate the brittle moth's lachrymosity. To fear the cargo within these pages, is to eke out a suspicious stun gun from the holy casserole of the Madonna. Zootropic humor drives us insane, and we wait for the inflated petunia. It's time.

Carlos Lara, author of *Like Bismuth When I Enter*,

winner of the 2018 Nightboat Poetry Prize

BLACK BALLOONS

Anthony Seidman

SPUYTEN DUYVIL

New York City

Some of these poems first appeared in slightly different versions in the following journals: AlligatorZine, Angel City Review Bitter Oleander, Blazing Stadium, Caesura, New, Loch Raven Review, Rio Grande Review, Slipstream, and Sulfur Surrealist Jungle. Much gratitude.

ISBN 978-1-959556-77-0

cover art : t thilleman (thillemantt.com)

Library of Congress Control Number: 2023942479

Para la Nylsa

Contents

To pacify loneliness, pick
a virginal day. Keep all your books
beneath seven locks. Carry an apple
beneath the purest tree. Have no fear,
the Evil one won't perturb you. Say
these words, as if they were
true: Loneliness,
I love you, I believe in you, don't abandon me.
Ernesto Mejía Sánchez

Loneliness Has Carbonized the Moon

If you dream you walk upside down, you will harvest plenty. If you dream loaded pistol, you are impotent. If you dream water, you will perish in a conflagration, most likely a jumbo jet. If you dream a great blaze, your teeth are loose, and you will sniff the opened container of turpentine your cuckold neighbor will ingest. In some regions, mostly tropical, the blind birds of desire twirl above the green canopies, enraged and shitting on the expanse beneath. Some say *that* implies greeting the anointed, and the common grave. If you dream teeth, the scarlet algebra of the bougainvillea. If you snore, snow and dark cabin. Every poem begins with prophecy or the washing of one's hands. Not all shrouds need be white. Worms take no accents into consideration when hungry. True, one could complain about only 80 or 90 years to breathe. That's wrong, though. Desert rises from her bed past noon, her boudoir is 120 degrees, and what good the basket of lemons if everything carbonizes?

PLASHINGS

Utter "rhododendron" and you lather the thighs of temptation. Rhododendron in scarf and teeth, in pink glove, bucket of ice and hammer. Rhododendron, plastic bags caught in a gust and mistaken for crows; rhododendron every Tuesday at 5:00 in the afternoon, sluggish pace of the mule beneath the carnivorous sun. Rhododendron in what tastes of October, water in a tin cup, aspirin, diesel exhaust and departure. In forklift and porcelain vase. Rhododendron in the drawing, perfectly rendered, of rhododendrons. Rhododendron, the drawing rubbed out. Fingers brushing away the bits of rubber and smudges. Rhododendron, erasure. Rhododendron, sore.

Evil

If you wish for strife in your neighbor's home, tie a red string around a fork and leave it in your pantry for seven days. Bury it beside the pink oleanders. If you wish to shame your son or daughter, cover your bedroom mirror with a black cloth, turn counterclockwise seven times, uncover the mirror and repeat the word *Bone-drip* five times. Laugh when you regard the one laughing at you. If you baptized Fire as Dentures; Cucumber as Shoe-Horn; Hemorrhoids as Morning Glory, and Jellyfish as Slash-and-burn farming, your sandals tread the path towards mastery. If you wish to win the lottery and share nothing, boil a live possum. If you wish to bear false witness: Cut your thumb and press your blood on the rear interior of soiled underwear. No one in this den judges you. It all starts with love. If you wish to lure your mistress when you're dying: have the nurse trap a moth in a mason jar and place it beneath your cot. Lover will arrive weeping and shearing her tresses. Sit up in bed. Sweating and breathless, point at her. Long hairs grow from her eyeballs.

CLODS

When I died—a long time ago—I was buried with wolf-fangs and transistor radio. While brain festered in my skull, I pondered negative numbers and the mess I had left: bills, some jottings reminding me to return a phone call from the black side of the sun. To gargle with laundry-detergent, as *mezcal* is now curated for silk cravats. A day later, I returned on the sly, peeking out the closet. When I died, they discovered fiction inside shoes I had left behind. The plumbers and auto-mechanics arrived, as they had been contracted weeks earlier. Aquatics, clogged. Sedan leaked ichor and plenty of soft jazz. I thought: enough with rats. Enough with the whiskers that sniff embryos. Supposedly there's water beneath the regolith on Mars. I sat up in my coffin before they could bury me. I was open arms. Stones gushed freely wherever a mansion stepped inside the camel who found a loophole through the needle's nostril.

Maggot Brain

The embryo-shredder. Disintegration of spiders. Trituration of toenails. Aspic on the blade. Gobs of flesh in a stainless-steel tray. Blood flecked on napkin. Wasp floating in a goblet of pinot grigio. Cough-lozenge-green dragonfly, two inches in length, skewered to the air vent of an SUV. Pus, warm. Smacked, mosquito stains adobe wall of the finca. Mercury bubbling. Load of semen in transparent tube. Fly rubs front legs then crawls across chunk of cheese sweating grease. Roadkill, possum, severed in two, twenty inches of entrail zigzagging across the asphalt. Hull of evacuated ootheca. Bovine livers in the butcher's stall; the non-gaze in the eyes of the cow's head on the cutting board. I was driving and the crow swooped in front of me; I heard the crunch and glimpsed in the rearview mirror at the beast flailing on the road. A rose mistaken for stab-wound. The folly of metaphor. Placenta, after stillbirth, and the stiff hare in a painting by Chardin. Bruise-blue and snot-yellow meat slab spat from the palette of Soutine. Viviparous, the newborn rattlesnakes writhe on dust, their venom, immaculate. Ice in the urinal. Touch nerve. Sniff the gangrenous. The amputated foot. My diabetic uncle, nearing death, seated by a fountain. His three remaining toes. Would only the foolish address them as the Trinity?

ATTRITION

Today the city spreads a fragrance of lemon. Rain, yellow or blue, but it tastes of leaf, stone. When someone dies an odor of vanilla takes hold of the air. Cities sweat vinegar and stale tobacco, or cherry cough syrup. During summer, heat glazes its sugar-cubes. Trees turn into amphorae containing wind or grain. That's when poetry flits and perches on the thin wires trilling from the laughter of children. The shadow retraces its step, crustacean, retrograde. Still, salt stings, open wounds never seal. Hunger unhinges, claws are honed, and the tombstone may prove too high for your hurdle.

Psychics Need No Zip Code

No one pulls the strings of a psychic's tongue. No one need crank the volume on the medium's hearing-aids. Some seers have veins in their eyeballs, branches of stolid oaks way past the graveyards. Others have whitest teeth, and they spread lips to speak crows, or hiss what you hear when pressing conch to your left ear to tune-in to the chilly chambers of the sea, drifting mariners and mirrors with blackened silver handles. Always a cliff's edge from tumbling into the breakers, you might as well pencil in your appointment. The ancient villages of black cauldrons and goons were torched ages ago. Long before apple pie and severance pay. Now cars rust at slower pace, although icecaps melt and aviaries house birds who no longer distinguish North from South. Some of the heartbroken embroider the absent lover on their pillow. Others invest in tractors or new boots to spit shine. Lovesick? Victim of scam? Not startled by the Crime Sheets or the Elections? Tired of eating too much electric blue but never sniffing Monet in your future? Don't worry. The psychics ask for no zip code. Foothills burn every summer. The ants remain ravenous. There's no friend to give you his shirt. Every minute, we're just a centimeter from the biggest blast, right?

The origin of red ants…dandruff and itchy armpit. The origin of wine…the hindquarters of a roan stallion. They took his toys away and he wept, he railed. The origin of sharks…the fluttering moth and insomnia, or twitching of nervous left foot. As an adult, they built a wall between his hands and lover. Her black hair turned into an octopus. That was the origin of pistol and obituary. The erasure of saurians with wing-spans like the red wood, an asteroid. The razing of cheap housing, linked to mushrooms and the thinning population of possums. The origin of mathematics: an eclipse, a legion of crabs covering the esplanade. After she died, he paused to hear the wind and voice of insects. He knew the ants were stitching a scripture of venom. The madmen sniffed and laughed. *Its ending is its origin,* he said, picking up a handful of mud to smudge a target in the center of his chest.

PREDICATED

You were born during a leaf storm, as a result you're adept at crossword puzzles. Mother made love to your father, and she dreamt nail-clippers and running down a tunnel that tapered to a needle's tip: this meant you would bully others. You already knew you shot blanks when your wife said: I'm pregnant. You were born during severe drought; hence, your preference for dim sum and off-track betting. The man you consider as your father loved cigars and cognac. He was infertile as a result of the mumps during childhood; your mother admitted to a tryst with the liquor-store clerk. You were born during spring…you can't resist fur or burnt sienna. You were born during the oil crisis, and debtors dunned you until your death at 53. The newlyweds thought a Vegas wedding was deliciously camp. She insisted they honeymoon in the wine-country. The night you were conceived Father had Super Bowl indigestion; you can't stand the sound of whistles. So much of what we taste, wear, or fidget has more to do with gloves, daybreak, unopened boxes, than not sleeping with our mothers.

Big Black

Shipwrecked alphabet; charred chassis of consonants scattered on the highway; garbage-heap of vowels; ants and green flies covering a gelatinous bone once a metaphor; gnarled bits of knowledge, ash, and burr sticking to a dead coyote's tail; the ecosystem of toxic toads, diphthongs; similes slit open with jagged razor; alone, the speaker wades a bog towards his cabin where sleep will sieve him into lilies, loins, slow fire black and blue, the etymology of dreams rewinding past the source of babble, mud. In his dreams, only there, the quill, the galleons of rum…the zipper…sample of steak-knives…umbrella, open.

Scratch Acid

My scab is a lake where bull shark flits towards chum;
my scab, a lion and the torn antelope; not just dried
blood, but ink crusted, and bubbles rising in a mug of
beer; my scab, the drift and suction-plunge upwards of
jellyfish; mitosis, thunderclap, and tarantula molting;
the glove folded inside out, my scab; the child staring at
the stuffed orangutan in the National History Museum;
my scab, his breath fogs the vitrine; my scab, knife
renting a nightgown in two; apotheosis in the junkyard,
one black galosh, and two sailors in a Turkish bath; my
scab everything that can be squeezed into an O, and
Ohhh, it's ovulating, orifice egging the oval exoskeleton
of the omniverse.

Tanka or Tonka

A tough choice, like betting on silkworms or the rambunctious crow. My uncle rode my BMX bike into the deep-end of the swimming pool on a lark. He left it there, much to the chagrin of my mother. He died penniless and attached to a ventilator, for one can't suck the oxygen from water. Cherry petals and the exuberance of spring still remind me of the worm, of dark waters where the ship-wrecked regard themselves in empty mirrors. I kept my toys outside, and the yellow tractors and trucks gathered sand in their axles. Yellow, the color of death, the color of old pages in a novel once read aboard hundreds of cross-continental jets. A charred fig tree. A missed tryst. The poetasters are painting ties and silk fans; they know toys rust. My father died last November, and I can't recall a thing about the leaves, the weather, the drizzle that did or didn't lick the asphalt black. I felt his death-rattle the way a spider detects a vibration on a silken thread. All of the calligraphy in this century can't cleanse me of his gnarled grip.

The Moon is Always Preterit

She escapes my ink. She escaped it long ago. Moon prior to human footprint and speculators. She offered no dowry but radiance to Marvell and his dew. To Tablada and his feverish cats in heat. To drunken Li Po. To moonslick shivering on the waters and Gorostiza's fisherman who dips net. What the moon projects on my opened hands is the light that escapes when I clench them. Nothing more than the phantom from the projection booth, dust-specks in abeyance. I preferred the weight of the orange in my palm to the fragrance, and a vacant lot to sunlight revealing the bougainvilleas and their crimson scripture. And now moon is textbook page or desert motel. Not the mirror and its Open Sesame. Not the river bursting my chest and churning into the estuary. Highway asphalt, semis, and neon. The din drags nails across my eardrums. Midnight, yet too much pollution to regard Her. Something about a bronze key tied to lavender ribbon. Something about a spiral staircase while I stare at Interstate 10. Diner's coffee, acrid. Within me: cool, long fingers turn the door-knob open.

As A Boy

I didn't read the classics. I read little, not much at all. But one must always do the right thing, like properly placing fork and knife atop plate when one has finished dining. Instead, I dreamt a caravel rocking over dunes, until my uncle or aunt occupied my breath and chided me, explaining how the music of the spheres exits only because of quotients set. Immemorial. Incorruptible. Now when I awaken at midnight to piss or sit in the dark I liken the window to a thousand lit torches within a cave so deep they cast no light. A river from childhood, a journey with no map. Or an island, shipwrecked. I hear, each night, the bonfires of warriors crackle on the shore with watchtowers in the distance. I sniff poems comparing thighs to a butterfly. All belong to the monologue on an adjacent stage, some rosebush emitting its fragrance in a bottle of perfume. And so, with chalk, blood, or ink in fist, I set forth, articulating the poem. The white gulls in the wind surge, and they shiver.

That Same Tune

Poem about three men in the same room. Or five men with bowler hats in the same literary salon and giant phonograph before them. Or poem about six women with blank eyes on the shore. None wear bathing-suits, for none have bodies. Only gauzy gush like waterfall beneath their faces. One woman discovers she is a shark. One man sits down on a stiff chair, another one walks towards the window, and he lights a cigar. Old recording crackles on the phonograph: could be jingle about shaving-lotion or dimensions of a ring orbiting Saturn. Another man siphons into medieval Bagdad. No civil strife, nor familial discord, must engender great poetry. But they congeal, at times. Especially if you have dead family members beneath the pink oleanders. Another woman laughs madly and finds herself on an assembly line, counting green bottles of beer. I woke up in the interrogation room, strapped to a metal chair. The mustache had yet to be waxed. Agent X and Strawberry complained about bathtubs and feral cats. In Helsinki or Bogota, the cats rouse a din when in heat, and the moon is deaf…perhaps even in cahoots.

It Seems Easy to Seduce the Distance

Don't be fooled. When others say "The Wind," or the "Vast Ocean," or even "Woman Beneath the Starlight," they prove mercantile. Hawking knickknacks at the Sunday swap-meet. Their prices include zeros, but they never press their ears against the emptiness, and their chatter doesn't sweat or claw. Others choose poetry, while some regard a bullet and ask if it contains enough soul to kill the one holding it up to the light. Either way, wind and ocean, and a woman in her black shawl is headed towards you, a retinue of moths and sluggish lizards following. Better polish your urn. Better start appreciating ash. Upon going mad one winter midnight, the sisters chained the poet to his bedroom window grille. I am born where you don't belong. I am the azure within its frame. Remember me when the wind tells you: I gave you stone.

Wow

Oaxaca in the busted wristwatch, in the sitcom; zombies, ash, drizzle; Oaxaca in the poet's wig, in the butcher's smile; Oaxaca, a bucket of fried chicken, a bottle of whiskey, and a blowjob; wow in Oaxaca and what in Oaxaca; I've never been to Oaxaca but I gotta' get some chapulines into my jig and jog, I gotta' duende my way out of the rut; Oaxaca, and the iguana takes one slow step; Oaxaca breathes fire and a syncretic stew; I lied,--I went to Oaxaca and lived on a diet of diphthongs, hammocks, and cheese; Oaxaca, ethanol and fireworks; Oaxaca, there is no tomorrow, no train through the looking-glass, but plenty of mudbasted sandals and incense; Oaxaca, I lack my pocketful of tokens, but the word Oaxaca pays for itself; the isthmus, Oaxaca, the crushed jungle and oxen, Oaxaca, pang of bliss, pupils dilated; Oaxaca the augmentation.

Soap

It is good to shave off your hair once. To shine the shoes of those amputated from beneath the knees. To whisper sweet little nothings in the ear of a deaf man, or to sit in the back seat of a junked sedan and await your chauffeur. A can of sardines past its expiration date or the first cockroach returning days since your last fumigation, and the Tragedian waxes his mustache. Thus, place burnt matches, clean underwear and socks in your knapsack. Bring a flashlight. The alphabet is dark and deep, and you'll need to bend beneath the stalactites. Surely beyond the traversal there's a clean and well-lit pub. You'll convince yourself to down some ale and swallow some shepherd's pie. If no starched tablecloth flutters after the crossing, rest assured there's a phantom, somewhere, awaiting your arrival. Look! There, perched on the branch of the black tree, the tremolo of five fingers waving, greeting you, deep within the torched orchards.

Insurrection

I wanted to celebrate. Confetti burst above me when I walked, my hands stained with the proof of regicide: off with the head of convention. Tourists seated on park benches replaced the judges. Each one, a septuagenarian blinking as an errant red ball bounced on the sidewalk. Fallen leaves rose up and covered the trees with hieroglyphs of birdsong. Billboards lowered like drawbridges and the avenues spread to a horizon with one clock-tower and black train hurtling towards the coast. I heard the Verb, basic as the fragrance from bakery, umbrage-laden highway, grain of pepper. Did it matter the misers would return? Clock hands would point again to midnight? Should I have withered while the ravenous roses inflicted wounds on the bountiful thighs of summer, thorns caught in her hair? Amid a confusion of ants and ash, I saw the evening, rain like a glistening curtain and, ajar, a door to the river.

Ferryboat Delayed While Waiting For Instructions

Love, when popped, stains something awful. Love secreted with skill is "milked" for ink, anti-venom. Ideally, love prepares a feast. In the morning, a fragrant white beard exclaims he's your bedfellow. Or were those crab-nebulae and quasars pounding inside your skull? Love, written in a font like pigeons or busted huaraches. The Two met at a flea market. The ferryboat was delayed. Islands everywhere, and metaphor equals sea-fare, or death, and sometimes desire. Friday means T-shirts as well, a cold beer and warding off the impending famine. He and They had 253 dollars together, and some matches. Both paid no attention to slatterns shrieking and pulling empty cans from the trash bin. Both had forgotten the tartness of the sea. Both possessed an oven in their gaze. Sometimes a couple bakes bread. Sticks together, eggshell to yolk. Sometimes, they part. One demonstrates mourning with spoonful of aspic.

Haiku or Hot-Cakes

You lack an epiphany like microwavable pizza. You want fifteen seconds, maximum, and a sudden arrival of gulls, or a cat slinking, paw after paw, from flower pots to the wooden floor where your slippers wait. I prefer to regard the hummingbird, neither here nor there, but in the moment. But I'm lying. There are no more hummingbirds on my urban block. Cherry blossoms. The mist mountain. The poet who drowned fishing the moonslick on the lake surface. I have more spare change than any sense of those tropes. How often do you awaken at dawn just to lick the dew? We all know you prefer sleeping in 'til noon.

CREW CUT

The origin of open windows...blue umbrellas and ribbons. The origin of delight...scissors, diorama of ant tunnels, zippers. Childhood remains something locked inside an empty DVD case. Adolescence sticks to one's fingers and making art out of paste and construction paper results in a telepathy not different from ice floes or microorganisms feeding a lake the color red. As a boy, he loathed piano lessons. Crows perched on the staves, and his thumb resting on middle C ached for iguana rainfall and steam rising from asphalt. The music he heard, an origin of hibiscus, or panther. When his father died, he remembered his son's birth. The skin, violet, flushed with redness. The origin of the death-rattle, infants bleating. When they took away his toys, he wept. He wanted the frigid dens of the deep. Ink spurting from startled octopi. The origin of kites: the weight of water. So much of street-mutt originates from blue whale.

Can I Follow Your Bones?

Or just your hearse, or the ink on your Last Will and Testament while the microwave's door is shut and a pound of ground beef defrosts? I open and close my balcony door, and a neighbor spits in his toilet, while the grammarian on the second floor above me peers out her spy-hole, concerned that the delivery of a dozen mangos and aspirin never arrived. I had reached a point with umbrellas and harpsichords and chondrites so that I swore I would never return to disco, pumpernickel bread, or wearing a T-shirt several sizes too short. But the metro car pulls in at the station, tires on a hotrod spin and burn rubber, and I am tempted to find myself behind the steering wheel of a coffin. Release me from clouds and mud. I am gripping the flowers in my gloves tonight, and I expect to reach the horizon in a second. Black balloon, fills with air. Bursts?

There Are No Heaths in Los Angeles

I've had it with mosquitoes, with clean porcelain, with shit, and even with starched napkins. Flexing my biceps—so laughable were you to regard them—I burst from my ootheca and screamed for Root Beer and Beef Jerky! All during hibernation I discovered a word called Disgust and it had lodged in my throat. My tomb, a cookie to dip in hot coffee. The dead ancestors, rain-coats jumping in front of the subway car. I have had it with ovens and ice-cream, with the genocide inflicted against microbes, with the poly-amorous play reserved for dogs, or a noose tightened for bald men or swimming-instructors. Urine has taken flight, and the white toilet reigns. But alone I haunt the butcher-shops. I hunt the matches and stable flames, the petrol spectators. It takes chutzpah to speak of time and space, and I am your humble servant. Significant cloud bares her breasts, lets fall a blouse knit from diesel and soft jazz, and her nipples are the keys opening the mirrors where the landscape smells of garlic, mint, and slowly, surely, you will discover the girl saved from the wolf's forest, for She's the one who wears feral language like a coat of thrashing raccoons, She's the hearth and the blade, and if the hut in the distance were explosive, surely, you would strike the door.

Eye, Hear

I hear a geography in my breathing, jungle beneath each fingernail, vacant lot tart with dust and sunlight, reek of ink and syntax, so foundational, like milk or gladioli. Verb Oh Verb, no more jeremiads about shipwrecks and fallen towers; the odor of semen from old tomes alliterates with dark gardens and fertilizes the feverish sleep of virgins. Verb is growing roots. Strophe ovulates. Couplet perks her breasts. Because my lungs, a landscape. Because my eyes, two lagoons. Because my limbs, a tarantula.

Seeds

You will die during a downpour because you cheated at cards and once opened a stranger's mail. Your molars will ache before the fever peaks. You will die while skiing: sudden blizzard, pine tree. That was the coda to your avarice, and abandoning wife and her tumor. You will die in your sleep during a nightmare because you failed middle school algebra. Prior to turning off the light, you placed your sneakers by your bed in case of an earthquake, just like normal. You will die during an earthquake beneath a collapsing overpass because of plate tectonics, and not because you loathed Wagner. One by one, keys are placed in the lock until something clicks. Your hair will start thinning a few months before you dream of the owl. You will see an owl on the night you die. Your son who suffers from aphasia will miraculously mention an envelope and scrabble game. Telescopes, hourglasses, and umbrellas: items you should collect in preparation. As a child you loved watching your father while he honed the kitchen knives. You will die surrounded by your family because you trapped a moth inside a mason jar. You also cheated at cards and once opened a stranger's mail.

KEROTAKIS

Now the Verb reaches me via conduits and commixtures: fruit of silence breaking flower into scarlet, cartilage and nerve, tamarind, lemon, sulfur, the opened triptych of thighs whose center panel sweats midnight. In this velvet one can't distinguish camembert from cabernet. Is that grease coagulating on the fields, redolent of garlic and mashed cilantro, or the blackest earth, indistinguishable from blood clotting, bull on hilltop, vinegar pouring on the valley? You Oh Verb rise from the tar. Heaven bubbles with stars and comets. I have levitated, float out the window among black roses, towards the hotel named after your toes. I am reading your hair and sniffing your accent of feverish fans and machetes. Rose of panties scrubbed with soap and left in the shower's stall. Rose of haunted mansions torched centuries ago. Rose of expired postage stamps and kite caught in oak branches. Rose of Rosa, whose name rhymes with everything molten and mortgaged, like atoms, train station, molasses, ivory. Bells, clanging?

Eyelids

For now, the coyotes breed. They disturb the trash. They kill the smaller breeds kept as lapdogs. The gardens shrivel because of drought. Some passers-by remember when October stung, because of chill, rusted nails. The toddler boy screamed; they had taken away his toys; he had tried to eat blue and plastic. Thirteen trains and their destinations chug along desire, and all of them are slippery, erect. Now that the toddler is eight, he boarded the caboose, and he slept in a rocking hammock above cases of gunpowder. Eyelids have a way of revealing desire. Sometimes Eros is a green wool sweater on an iron hanger. Sometimes, what you have been waiting for: red stage, empty armchair, and the one who abandoned you for the wind, or confetti, or a jeroboam filled with milk. None of that makes you less earth, less stone, less fire, and less sugar. But the other one hinges on doe slippers, finely ground coffee, the pen still jutting from the robe's breast-pocket.

Proscription

What fits in the right hand is meant for the sinister: a crow's feather, a hollow ootheca, and a handle to the door that doesn't open. Shutters bang in the mind's attic, and the ceramic doll has opened her eyes. Outside, metallic animosities are shredded by dogs, and a tractor in a ragged field sits idling, its engine on for hours, no one at the wheel. Detective or Arsonist, you who awaken to this tableau, remind the Dreamer to stay asleep, sweating in his bed while moths cough from the mudcaked boots placed beside the scissors and parcel, for the Black Raincoat now pauses at his front door, deciding which glove will deliver the summons.

Shall We Play a Game?

If you wake up on your left side, your shoes will last the day. Black sedan will not be parked in front of the doughnut shop where you buy coffee. If you wake up on your right…best speak of rivers, fedoras, and dusk. Don't bend over to pick up a penny. No luck there. If you end the day with pennies in your pocket, throw them in the trash. The result: a restful night, no indigestion. If your spouse falls asleep face-up: comet showers, frayed slippers, dislocated shoulder. If you start your day by stepping forward with your right foot and have yet to sneeze, the rain has been delayed. If your zipper snags, well, you will not attend tomorrow's parties. No more champagne for you! Of course, if you toss a quarter and ask: Heads or Tails? You have been indoctrinated into the wisdom of thin paint on dry-wall. You're exuding the skills of man eating pasta with a single chop-stick. Let's save departure for twilight; the lute's string has yet to be plucked. Let's reserve snail, orange, and cognac. If you step outside your front door and no crow, siesta awaits you. You shall be fruitful, despite your aversion to wash-cloths. Despite dandruff.

No Gold Mine

Life working the cash register inside a mini-mart does not blossom jukebox and beer-tap. But you find yourself bogged there. No need to claim responsibility. Red is the color of corn. Blue is the hue of sacrifice. Violet, blood of the warrior. You're no warrior, despite the fact that your uniform employs those three colors. Remember Kafka, whom you may have never read, and his noonday nightmares. Or Dali and lobster-tigers barfing an odalisque. You will escape one day into the forest where you will find old cauldrons and the cook books once thumbed by Goons. You will make your way to the other side; break on through. Even if it means hiding in the attic of an abandoned farm house. Seek a hearth beyond the trees. Check that the oven's iron and lit. We will remember you that first night when you snore atop a goose-feather-stuffed pillow. I will have left you a reminder on the front-door: Green is the color of festive feathers. Rent is paid in Black; obsidian, the color you will use to kill.

MOTHER AND CROW

Mother doesn't wish to hear the voice of her dead son. Mother must, mother will. At night, the mountain lions and coyotes descend, sniffing fish fried with olive oil in heavy pans, the red chambers of lust, trash cans full of love notes and grease bags of French-fries. Mother sweats asleep. In her sleep, she locks herself inside a room containing nothing but a chair painted blue and gold-fish in bowl atop a coffee table. The room turns black. Mother doesn't wish to hear weeping. She wants her anguish back and to stuff it inside her purse. But mother must, and mother will listen to the carpenter nailing fresh wood. Mother weeps, trees shiver. Cats retreat, rain commences. Crows strut on night grass, long beaks picking peanut shells, candy wrappers. Now the clouds caw.

Dead Letter Office

Without metaphor, no drought nor mud. Rain becomes simple aerobics. No odor of jacarandas and summer evening opening her syrupy jaws. Without metaphor, plain milk and cookies. A yawn can be a thorn, or genocide, or C Major 7th chord played on a Casio keyboard from 1984. Fish break apart. Left-handed accountants discover they're talented at softball, but they no longer probe wires into the tar-pits sealing the tax-codes from ages Jurassic and ambidextrous. No motive to speak of green and electric things. The young woman who is now a raving beauty will settle for olives and spanking-new German sedan. And the nobody now a Someone, picks a canapé with salmon and cream-cheese from a silver platter. He's the Guest of Honor. The pill he concocted promises no more indigestion. Estrogen has returned to being simply that. A knife still cuts, but mainly bread or steak. A drunkard in some distant tavern is crying…something about his heart breaking, though we now know hearts simply cease.

Border Psycho

My wristwatch fills with rain. A sarcophagus and tsunami walk together holding hands. Sometimes a fern can grow from the toilet, or a Verb can plunge into the gutter and then reach the sea. I never tasted honey until I was fifteen, and by then I thought cinnamon was poison. With engineering so faulty, I will never know the exact hour. So I have decided to pump gasoline into my heart and ingest a lit match. That means I will reach you within an instant. The black dog with a blue leash tied to a street-lamp will run around it, run and run around it, until the leash gets entangled or snaps. Obscure are the currents that reach my ears after midnight. I am drowning but breathe with the ease of a dream gargling murder.

Fur For Fear

Birth, an odor of vanilla and rust. Sometimes the color blue licks the city and, summer, omniscient. Inside the tent of an armpit, a new mother remembers that fireworks inscribe bougainvilleas and their algebra in the night-sky. Stop begging for bread, stop weeping when the ferryboat has gargled diesel, its engine puttering across the lagoon towards a cabin and tobacco. Baptism takes place tomorrow, at the hour of a crow and tarantula. Everything, foundational. There is no verb without tired feet, no tired feet without the alphabet, no alphabet without the hunter, no hunter without the gun and the target, and the target is the gun that becomes the hunter's spine as his rifle aims at his own geography of breathing.

Filling the Bag

I fill my name with the names of others, their social security numbers, their allergies, predilections for pistachio or pesto, their nightmares, and dental records. I live on the side of every road leaving the darkest counties with no mayor, an empty library, and two whiskey bars for each neon church. I stick my thumb out and board a big-rig or a rusted sedan and pass cornfields or desert expanses before reaching the gas station where I inquire about the distant lights, walk the mile, and fill my ever-filling bag with narratives and house keys, photo albums from the 80's, and the CD collections of widows in love with Hair Metal. But what good is all that junk? My bag drags. Has proved impossible to lug. Cars whiz past my thumb. My brain has become a wilderness. My tongue, something spoken by crows or cockroaches. I fill my bag—my love— because my shopping cart is lacking your curve and perfume. They're shutting down the lights in this mega-mart. Midnight spits headlights and road-rage on the highway. Parking lot, empty. Tell me where you have gone. Tell me please, as my bag is now empty, and I am at the roadside where strays, the unhospitable, and raincoats await the chemistry of ghosts,

the un-curable cough of diesel, and a feral roof.

Why Moon Rhymes With Spoon

If you nick your neck while shaving, you will encounter a gold coin among the wreckage in your top desk drawer. If you smell vanilla spreading over the city, someone's father has died. This happens often, like nasal congestion or dinosaurs. You will sleep better that night, knowing you still can rip meat when it's snatched fresh from the grill. If you discover a can of sardines in your pantry, a year past expiration date, bury it beside the pink oleanders. This means your child will become a baker. If you decide to shave off your hair, or cover a mirror, you will find you have much in common with the red woods or the sea sponge. They are regarded as nature's best survivors. If you still care why moon rhymes with spoon, or with June, moon also rhymes with forty, mortgaged, gunpowder, lemon, or ink. The white gulls in the wind surge, and they shiver.

You're So Vein

You walk shirtless, and the day, overcast. You put on a red sweater and ear-muffs,--a sudden heat-wave. You lack sugar,--salt on the table. You pine for a mango, and the butcher sharpens his knife, wipes hands on stained apron. You ask for aspirin, and a chalice of Soda-Pop reaches you on silver platter. Cabal places watch-tower on the chessboard. Dogs growl when they sniff your after-shave. Why does the tree, rigid and Oak, follow you? Whenever you turn around, it's only a yard behind you. Branches: claws. Bark gray as twice-used funeral shroud. You chew bubble-gum, a black balloon bursts. Ever spin a globe and stop it at random with your finger? That's where you don't belong. A furrow that smiles like an open grave. This poem is about Kleenex, about the motives for wearing gloves and eating more fiber. When your lover breaks up with you a third time, she repeats: *Just imagine the fourth!*

Each tribe considered themselves the true people. *Yąnomamö* means "human being". Lugal-zagc-si reigned over Umma, Sumeria. The god of storms, Enlil, anointed Him. His throne extended across the known world: five hundred miles. Tenochtitlan, navel of the cosmos according to the Mexica. Times Square during the 1940's: if you slowly sipped coffee at the Automat, the Milk Way was believed to rotate around you. The neon outside smelled of sweat and liquor. What can't be expressed in words, let alone music? Does the lack of articles in Latin make each noun heavier? Is the subjunctive mood expendable? The Name that can't be uttered, although Moses saw His sandaled feet and backside. We felt we had bull's-eyes on our chest, learning too late that we had sinned. The prisoners were decorated. Some played flutes. 42 children sacrificed to Tlaloc to ensure rain and bountiful crops. They were slowly immolated so tears would quench the God. Witnessing a doe among the meadow flowers, the hunter couldn't raise his rifle. It was the hour of the evening breeze when we heard Ha-Shem walking in the garden. On his last or first foray, the archer unleashed an arrow. The arrow didn't budge.

BAD TENANTS

Leaving too early, slamming doors past midnight. Radios in their eyeballs, blasting. Rumored to have been the Goons boiling toads and bile in the black cauldrons deep within forests now carbonized. The Verb needs rent paid, or late-fees accumulate and loam will no longer alliterate with lyre. They're feeding their children clouds and comet-showers, while you're on a strict budget of lettuce and gutter. Other possible tenants arrive with letters of recommendation, wax seals, signets as valuable as functioning pancreas. They glimpse water-stains on the ceiling, and move on to better cages. Some even find an apartment with balcony in center of the letter Zero. Your watch is flooded. No room for orchids and a couplet to seal the deal. Now an odor of chocolate permeates the city. That means several births, at least, not to mention the courtship rituals of mosquito. Disinherited, the poet dreams of teeth. The landlord barfs a new alphabet. When metaphor fries a patty at the right temperature, it means just that.

Why Desire Rhymes With Fire

A fragrance of strawberry pervades the city and syntax turns aquatic. Now wine pours blue and rinses mud from eyes buried in work-boots. This means a season of coitus. The couple flutters past the purple curtains of their window, and the great thumb and forefinger pins their flame-tinctured wings against the moon. Fireflies now inhabit caryatids. Lighthouse at the tip of cigarette. Sphinx holding a bouquet of roses and the mantra of the staircase and garret which brims over with the fragrance of fruit. The boy scribbled plum and sky against the white construction paper. Scribbled and the paper opened. Lianas, bewitched. A weather like syntax became humidity. Words proved to be water, and just as ambulatory. The boy was laughing. The jilted bride picked up the pillow with His name embroidered. She put the pillow to her ear. Heard an alarm-clock ring. The white gulls in the wind desired, then expired.

Nowadays

The white crow, like the black rose, would have fared better in a cage. The last Dodo passed through the digestive tract of a Dutch sailor in the late 1600's. The birds didn't fear humans and couldn't fly. The meat was closer to pork than chicken. So much of beauty resides in what is distant or extinct. The child grabs at a slant of light, dust-specks pirouetting. The man approaching fifty now yearns for the breasts he never caressed. When Mexican Marxists and Anarchists volunteered for the Sandinistas, they found themselves in a jungle. They ran out of provisions. But the region abounded in iguana. When you first chew iguana meat, it tastes of chicken, followed by rank seafood. *De gustibus non.* The married woman experiences strict pleasure during a tryst with a woman ten years her senior; her husband plans their anniversary, unawares. A century after the Church was established, the last naiad was found bathing in the Jordan River. Twelve hunters threw down their bows and arrows, exclaiming: *Her beauty is perfect!* The greater number of men insisted: *Kill her!*

The Sun is Conditional

The galaxies expand at two thousand twenty miles per hour. If the speed of light results in a sailor's Glad Eye, all the better. Alphabets expand and contract, then a Vowel impregnates some camel, lake, or thunderous night. The Sun has always waxed his mustache. And when he returns from his business trip, he will open our knapsacks and count all the candy we have hidden, while we listen to his stories of Southern heat and the spider spitting from each wave on the beach. Bastards will remind him how no flowers bloom without smoke, or how a basement inside the stomach possesses a microphone recording the subpar plumbing. But we seek the stomach within the stomach, the father within the thumb. The white gulls shiver, because my lungs, tarantula. The pale son arrives at a field full of dung; he smears some on his forehead. Some mammal coughs up its last breath. We would dance on the surface of the sun. We would splash fire through our teeth.

Anthony Seidman is a poet and translator, born and raised in Los Angeles, and who has spent significant stretches of his life living in Ciudad Juarez and Mexicali, Mexico. He currently resides in the San Fernando Valley with his wife, author Nylsa Martinez, and his two children. His most recent books include *That Beast in the Mirror* (Black Herald Press: London-Chartres), a bilingual gathering of his poetry with translations rendered into French by poet Blandine Longre, and *Cosmic Weather* (Spuyten Duyvil, New York). Cardboard House Press published his translation of *Contra Natura* by Rodolfo Hinostroza in 2022, and additional poems, translations, reviews, and articles have appeared in such journals as Latin American Literature Today, Ambit, New American Writing, Los Angeles Review of Books, Poetry International, Rattle, as well as in literary magazines from Chile, Argentina, and Mexico.

www.ingramcontent.com/pod-product-compliance
Lightning Source LLC
Chambersburg PA
CBHW021346060726
47591CB00006B/2178